Life is a Ball
Don't Put Me in a Box

By Mira Stulberg- Halpert
©1-776242971 2012

Illustrations by: Caroline Maynard

Mira Stulberg-Halpert

Life is a Ball

Hello!

I'm Mira Stulberg-Halpert, MEd and have devoted my professional life to helping all students succeed and feel empowered by WHO they are.

I developed an alternative learning program, called 3D Learner, to initially help my own children achieve success when naysayers said it was not possible. I help students and their families understand how they think and learn, which can be creative and unique. They don't always attain the level of success needed in the standard molds created by our educational system.

My passion and belief is that EVERY child can succeed. When given the tools that center on their strengths as well as the opportunity to use their abilities, these issues that have historically held them back, can be strengthened and success can be achieved.

No specific medical/psychological labels are applied to these children: labels can sometimes take a parent down a long and confusing road. Instead, I view these 'kids' (even as adults, their nature is childlike and fun-seeking) as individuals who think DIFFERENTLY. If we look at their abilities and view them in a different light, their individual potential can be realized! This is true for those identified as intellectually gifted as well as those who may be developmentally delayed.

**They are Balls in a world full of boxes…
who make up the rules!**

Mira Stulberg-Halpert

"Life is a Ball, Don't put me in a Box" was written so that parents, grandparents and professionals can view their child, grandchild and student from a strength-based perspective. I wrote it in a DIFFERENT format so that those reading it might gain some insight into understanding what it is like to LEARN DIFFERENTLY. It is meant to be shared—just as these children are meant to be celebrated for WHO they are and what is possible for them to achieve. It is our responsibility to see that we give them the right opportunity to BOUNCE as HIGH as they can - and not DEFLATE their enthusiasm or their potential.

If after experiencing "Life is a Ball", you recognize traits that are your child's, I hope you will seek the support your child desperately needs to be happy, creative and successful in school and life. As parents, we hold the keys to unlock that potential...use them wisely.

Mira "The Success Mom"

Life is a Ball

> "Today you are You, that is truer than true. There is no one alive who is Youer than You."
>
> —Dr. Seuss

Mira Stulberg-Halpert

Life is a Ball

Hey Mom (and Pops too) I'm talking to you
Are you pulling your hair out and don't know what to do?
Here you've got this child - your pride and joy
He's driving you crazy - seems he likes to annoy.

It could be your daughter, 'cause girls are this too
Whatever it is, they don't think EXACTLY like YOU!

I am sure you never thought that the way they think
Could actually lead you to the edge of the brink.

Well, I'm here to tell you to just calm down
And relax and smile instead of fret and frown
You need to rejoice and REALLY stand TALL
For it is very possible that your child's a BALL!

If Mothers and Fathers lead the way
Then all our kids can have a better day

So please join my call for one and for all
Let everyone know It's OK to be a ball.

It's really not hard to help your child be successful
But it's important to know that waiting is dreadful
Every day that you wait to help your kid thrive
Is one more day they just try to survive.

So let's make it TODAY that you decide
To help your child make a great stride.

Once you finish this book
I think you'll be hooked
That having a ball is part of the fun
If you're lucky enough to nurture one.

So from one parent to another the last thing I'll say
I'm grateful my kids were balls —
I wouldn't want it any other way!

Mira Stulberg-Halpert

Life is a Ball

In the beginning...

From the beginning of time, God made us all
But I really believe he created us FIRST as balls.
We were playful and curious and full of content
Truly understood life and knew what it meant.

Other objects were made to be by our side
They were smooth and flat and had nothing to hide.
But balls were needed to explore and find life
While the others were there to support us in strife.

For way back then, we had to survive
And if you were flat, it was hard to thrive
One had to be free and able to roam
and not sit around or be alone.

Balls had to be able to think very fast
To explore our world, which was still so vast.

And soon there were many more balls around
Who now felt it was time to settle down
Some felt it important to communicate
So they made silly symbols as their first template.

They interacted with each other and made up this code
and rules to follow when they weren't on the road.

But the groups of these balls who sat around
Just looked at each other and started to frown
They sat around so long they began to flatten
Nobody knows just how this all happened

Mira Stulberg-Halpert

As the younger balls rolled into this place
The flattened ones taught them the rules they'd face.
Soon these rules were taught and recorded somehow
And those that made them - ruled now.

These rule makers gave themselves a name
"We'll call ourselves boxes – and make the others ashamed".

While there were many balls that went out exploring
(because sitting around to them was just so BORING)
They still felt the need for discovering and creating
While boxes were home learning writing and reading!

When these balls returned, they felt like fools
Now THEY had to abide by the boxes rules
They had ALWAYS been creative and smart
But now the world they were in was totally dark.

And they had to learn a whole new way
It seemed to them they had no say.

As time went on large schools were built
And boxes continued to hand out the guilt.

These schools still remain today
And balls still feel like they're in the way.

Life is a Ball

Being Different is OK

So if in fact life is a ball
Then flattening us out should not be the call
As teachers and parents and coaches abound
Shouldn't we strive to keep these balls round?

'cause when we are born, we're much the same,
Round, bouncy and ready for life as a game.
We're happy and full of hope for the future
Our family and friends are thrilled - that's for sure!

The first part of our life is really fun
We roll and bounce - we even run!
But something happens as we get older
That 'something' gets in the way, and we get bolder.

That boldness is sometimes abruptly cut short
As boxes around give us 'logical' support.

We roll around without much care
We bump into things with lots of flare
We're always searching and asking WHY?
But boxes responses often make us cry.

And then we are called some very bad name
And run off in a tantrum, feeling WE are to blame.

Mira Stulberg-Halpert

Life is a Ball

Learning to read seems the hardest for us
For we can't seem to learn like others think we must!

Reading phonetically might work for some
But for balls it seems incredibly dumb
Now don't get me wrong, it's important to know
That certain letters make sounds — like the T and an O.

But what if those sounds don't make any sense
Haven't you noticed how your child gets tense?
So why do we insist on this "drill and kill"
Just because some studies say we ALL need this skill?

It's amazing to me that after all this time
We make non-phonetic readers feel like they've committed a crime.

The more creative they are the harder it is
To LOOK at an "I" and pronounce it an (ĭ) …like in wish.

If learning to read was like a game
There'd be lots of balls in the HALL OF FAME.

Mira Stulberg-Halpert

For them learning to read like others seems LAME
Especially when they feel they're in the HALL OF SHAME!

There are ways to teach reading that might seem unique
And to others it might seem like that teacher's a 'freak'
But when balls look at letters of words as a whole
And they understand what it MEANS, they're in control.

Because words create pictures in our own minds
And without them any meaning is hard to find.
It's important that words make a movie in our head
Or else we don't understand what we just read.

We come is all sizes, but one thing's for sure
We're meant to be balls, not things boxes can cure
In my experience of working with balls I have found
It's really quite hard to remain a ball and stay round.

Because we live in a world where boxes rule
I find we don't work with the same set of tools.

Alas, we don't get that until one hits the wall
And has to recover from a very bad fall.
As we look around and realize we're not all quite the same
Because sometimes adults are too quick to fix blame.

Life is a Ball

From the time we are born to the time school starts
It's amazing how others think we are SO SMART!
We rattle off songs and poems galore
And people keep shouting they want to hear more
We dazzle and frazzle them with our charm
And make every animal sound in the barn.

You know I was a genius until I was four
Then they made me learn rules and I said "NO more"
We take apart things with lightening speed
And build Lego® structures that everyone needs.

When playing games us balls are as smart as a fox
But because we can't read we're as "dumb as an ox"
When we go to places where we've never been
It's amazing how well we remember them!

Mira Stulberg-Halpert

Quite often folks say balls are unmotivated and lazy
Those comments make balls feel like they are just crazy!
There are some of us balls that are clumsier than others
Though not always the case — take the Ringling Brothers!

There are many who are dare devils and good at "extreme" sports
For them flipping on skateboards never puts them out of sorts.
It's unfortunate that we label many top athletes as "dumb"
If we used their talents to help them learn - you'd be stunned.

There are so many abilities that these students possess
Yet the rest of the world makes them feel they have less
Intense, sensitive emotional, smart
Sometimes they're good at music and art.

Life is a Ball

Material that's too easy is really a bore
The more complex it gets is NOT a chore
It's difficult puzzles that excite the most
But "drill and kill" assignments turn balls into ghosts.

Balls have the keen ability to be imaginative and creative
As well as the energy and excitement to take every moment to live.

Although we're not great at logical and sequential deeds
We make up for those traits with our own creed.

If we have an idea of what's expected
We find our own way that's never been tested.
To be a ball is lots of fun
Even if we don't learn like everyone.

Mira Stulberg-Halpert

Balls need DIFFERENT ways to learn the best
But once we "get it" we're better than the rest.
Since balls are round, we can move very fast
Yet once in control, we can be a blast.

Balls can move without much impetus
Which of course makes boxes around us – furious!
But reading and writing are for balls a bad dream
It can make us so angry that we want to scream.

We're often scolded for not being attentive in school
But the mountain of pictures in our heads makes sitting still not so cool.
Listening to directions is not really our thing,
All those words create noises that make our brains just go "BO-RING!"

Life is a Ball

The way we learn best is to SHOW us how
We visualize and experience and it makes us go WOW!
We know that it's not how most teachers teach
But we're students too and we want to be reached!

It's very important that the world understand
That balls can be successful if given a hand.
For it is boxes and balls that need to work together
To make sure that EVERYONE learns to make the world better.

The world needs boxes to have a stable base
But must nurture us balls who need some extra space.
For if it weren't for balls rolling about in a haphazard way
We'd still be sitting in the dark and eating curds and whey.

Mira Stulberg-Halpert

Life is a Ball

It is not to say that boxes only use words and balls do not,
It's just when balls need to use grammar, those sentences are shot.
Hey - let's look at the way that I've written this book
Punctuation and grammar are certainly off the hook!

What the world needs most — and that's not a lie
Is a combination of a box and a ball that tries.
When a ball and a box learn to understand each other
They may realize that we actually NEED one another.

It is not correct that only boxes rule
Or that balls roll around aimlessly and think they are cool.
Thinking "out of the box" should be the ideal
But if you're a ball - that goal is already real!

There needs to be a way that sticks
For balls and boxes to co-exist.
For if we don't, and at this task we fail
Then lots of progress will fade and go pale.

And that's OK if we want to live in the past
But our world today is moving too fast.

It's CALM, CONFIDENT and POSITIVE SUPPORT that we need
We can do it together to help plant the seed.
For future students don't ever have to fail
We will be positive role models on every trail.

Mira Stulberg-Halpert

The fighting and teasing has got to stop
Or else our kid's future will certainly drop.
And parents please remember I'm your kid too
Even if … I think different than you!

There are so many things that we can do
To make our kids feel special and successful too.
So watch out world….LIFE IS A BALL
And we should live it…for ONE and FOR ALL!!

Life is a Ball

My Confession!

I'm here to announce to one and to all
That I, for one, am proud to be a ball.
It certainly wasn't always this way
And being different, was hard, I must say.

The problem of course is it's not always fun
To be picked on and blamed for not getting things done.

The worst of course was when I first went to school
That's when I thought I was incredibly cool.
I had no idea what the teacher was saying
So instead of listening, with my pencil I started playing.

My teacher's response was really quite shocking
It sounded to me like an elephant honking!
I'm really not sure exactly what was said
But remember wanting to hide my head.

It was soon after that I realized something was wrong
And I needed to do something to show I was strong.
I told my teacher right then and there
That I thought that she looked – oh – rather square!

I realize now that that was probably not smart
But IT was that moment that gave ME my START!!
The belief that "YES INDEED I AM DIFFERENT" and thank goodness for that
I believe that I am round—and certainly not FLAT!

Mira Stulberg-Halpert

I pondered that thought for a little while
And soon began to let my imagination run wild.

After many years of working with these wonderful creatures
This theory of roundness developed unique features.

Once you embrace that these possibilities in fact do exist
You find that your admiration for these kids (and adults) you can't resist.

Please explore the possibilities of your child's potential
And your rewards you'll find will be exponential.
As I've tried to explain how balls may think and learn
I hope you will support them, and their trust you will earn.

Life is a Ball

Testimonials!

"As a parent we often wonder if we are doing the right thing for our kids, and I know that sending him to your program was essential. I look at him now and wonder what if I did nothing? How different would his future be if I didn't act and just allowed him to continue to struggle and become further demoralized."
— Sandra M., Delray Beach, Florida

"I want to thank you and your family at 3D Learner for being such a wonderful answer to prayer!

You have made a lasting impression on my grandson, and have given my daughter the tools she needs to work with him. You and Mark are true advocates for children who are trying to find their voice.

May you be richly blessed in the days ahead."
— Marilyn C., Franklin, Tennessee

"Thanks for keeping us in-the-loop!! Our son has made incredible leaps and bounds this academic year. As a result of his own personal growth and maturity, his work with 3-D Learner and an incredibly skilled and dedicated educator; he has not only met, but exceeded my expectations! I am incredibly proud of him."
— Stephanie M., Boca Raton, Florida

Mira Stulberg-Halpert

"*Our daughter had a fantastic 6th grade year at the middle school. I know that so many of lessons we learned from you along with the reading program played a large part in her success.
I felt like I was one step ahead of everything after going through your program. There are so many kids out there that could benefit from your program.*"
— Michelle R, Surfside Beach, SC

Life is a Ball

"*I just wanted to drop you a note about our son.*

He is making straight A's, reads on his own, loves to read, tells us all about the stories he reads, does his homework at aftercare, has been put into a program called TOT (Teachers of Tomorrow) where he reads to Kindergarten kids and helps them learn to write, has already gotten a citizenship award at school, and the teachers tell us he is THE BEST STUDENT they have ever had, model student, role model to the other kids, and the nicest and sweetest kid they have ever had, has an SRI reading score of 800 (average they say is 650?), has scored a 3 on both math and reading FCAT practice tests..... I guess I could go on, but I think you get the point.

I know there are a number of factors that have contributed to this success, and I strongly believe that the number one factor is from the time he spent with you guys! It can't be a coincidence!

He is so proud of what he is doing and we appreciate everything you did for him! Thanks so much!"
— Dave and Kim L, Boynton Beach, FL

Mira Stulberg-Halpert

>"Mira:
>
>Six years ago we had the pleasure of having you work with our son. I thought you might like to have an update.
>
>Our son will be graduating from HS next Saturday. He had an IEP until his senior year when his test results found that he no longer qualified for spec. ed. and was not to be covered under the 504. He has taken college pre-course all through HS and his senior year took honors level course. He will be attending the Vt. Tech. College in the fall to study Civil Engineering.
>
>When I asked him what helped him throughout his education, your technique with the 3D Learners is always mentioned. He has also perfected the Wilson Reading Program, but he feels one without the other would not have made him as successful as he has been.
>
>Thank you for being a part in his success."
>— Nancy S., NH

Life is a Ball

This is what a student had to say about his experience at 3D Learner

"I enjoyed going to 3D Learner. The days went really fast and I didn't want to go home on Friday. Everything about the program was fun. It's working really well, because all I have to do is picture the word in my head and spell it. I wish that the 3D Learner was 2 blocks away from our house because then we could go there often and the weather wouldn't be so hot. I used to have hard days at school, but now they are good. School is much better and easier after going to 3D Learner."
— Robert G., Juneau, AK

Final word….

I've been blessed by a gift to be able to write
Maybe not in the way that you think is right.
But words have meanings that are vivid for me
I can see them in my mind just as clear as can be.

It is just this gift that God's given to me
That I want to share with the world — so all can be free,
The biggest gift of all that I can give to the earth
Is to have children be happy and move freely from birth.

It is movement and vision and love and support
That is all that is needed to be a good sport.

I'm not asking for much for this gift in return
All I ask is your help so that all kids can learn.
There's only one way that this dream can come true
And it ultimately comes down to just me and you.

Be they boxes or balls or something in between
We need to reach out and on each other lean.
If we stop pointing fingers and handing out labels
We might actually realize that these kids are QUITE ABLE!

To come up with ideas that have never been proven
To end world hunger or stop air pollution!
We'll never quite know just what they might do.
Unless we support them - and then follow through.

Life is a Ball

It is my fervent hope that with these words
Many will realize our education system is absurd
Our children desperately need our help
In every corner of the world this need is felt.

So hug your child and heed this call
It's very important to nurture one and all.
And if your child happens to be a ball
Then do something about it - it's so worth the call!!!

It is up to us to make the difference in their lives.

Do it NOW -- before their SPIRIT dies.

Oh… there is one more thing I forgot to mention.
I want to hear your story for the next edition.
Your story of LIFE IS A BALL — yes I want to share it
So parents everywhere can know they can bear it!!!!!

Call me today before it's too late.

For your child's sake – there's no time to wait.

Mira Stulberg-Halpert

Contact Mira at

561.361.7495

parents@3dlearner.com

For more information and a free assessment

www.3DLearner.com